A Very Special Day

Teresa couldn't wait to get home. It had been a very special day at school. Teresa's best friend, Katie, had a new baby sister. Katie's dad, Mr. Murphy, had come to school to tell Katie the good news. Mr. Murphy brought candy for the whole class and the afternoon turned into a celebration. Everyone wanted to know what name Katie's parents had given her new baby sister. Mr. Murphy whispered in Katie's ear. All the children had shouted out, "Tell us, Katie. Tell us!" Katie told everyone they would have to guess.

Some of the guesses were really funny and everyone laughed and laughed. Finally, Joe who sat way in the back guessed, "JoAnne." Katie nodded yes and everyone clapped.

Mr. Murphy took Katie back to the hospital with him so she could meet her new sister. It took a while for things to calm down. Then Mrs. Edwards, Teresa's and Katie's teacher, told everyone to take out their crayons and markers because they were going to make a WELCOME banner. Mrs. Edwards explained that she would drop the banner off at Katie's home after school so Katie and her dad could hang it up to welcome home Katie's mom and JoAnne.

Teresa shared the good news with her mom after school. Teresa was also curious to know if there had been any celebration when she was born. Teresa's mom smiled and gave her a big hug. She told Teresa how filled with joy everyone had been and how much they knew she was a gift from God. Teresa wanted to know if her family had celebrated the way she had in school with her classmates. Teresa's mom went to the drawer where all the family photos were and took out some pictures. As she handed the pictures to Teresa, she told Teresa all about her Baptism celebration. She explained when Teresa was only a few months old, she and Teresa's dad, Teresa's

Godparents, Uncle Tim and Aunt Pam, and their whole family had taken Teresa to church. At church the priest, Father Bob, had poured water over her head saying, "I baptize you, Teresa, in the name of the Father, and of the Son, and of the Holy Spirit." When Father Bob had finished baptizing Teresa, everyone clapped their hands as a way of welcoming her into the family of God.

When Jesus walked this earth he spoke about God in a new way.

Many wondered who this person Jesus could be. When they asked who he was, Jesus said, "I am the Good Shepherd."

Jesus told them how the sheep are very special to the Good Shepherd. He knows each sheep by name. When the sheep hear the Good Shepherd's voice, they know him and want to be with him. The sheep run away and will not follow a stranger because they do not recognize his voice.

The Good Shepherd goes before his sheep. He does not go behind them and scold them along; he goes in front to show them the way.

The Good Shepherd knows all the needs of the sheep. He gives them green grass, fresh still water, exercise, and a sheepfold where they sleep protected at night.

The Good Shepherd gives all his love, time, and attention to the sheep. He lays down his very life for the sheep.

See John 10:3-15

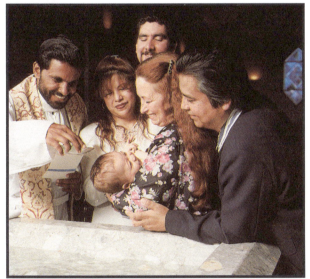

The first sacrament you received was Baptism. A sacrament is a sign of God's love for us.

Your family wanted you to become a member of God's big family, the Catholic Church, and so they brought you to church to be baptized. It is through Baptism that we become children of God.

Since your Baptism, your family has helped you grow in God's love. The Church also helps you and your family grow in God's love.

The waters of Baptism remind us that we have been saved from our sins and we are free to grow in God's love. This is also the beginning of our new life with Jesus Christ.

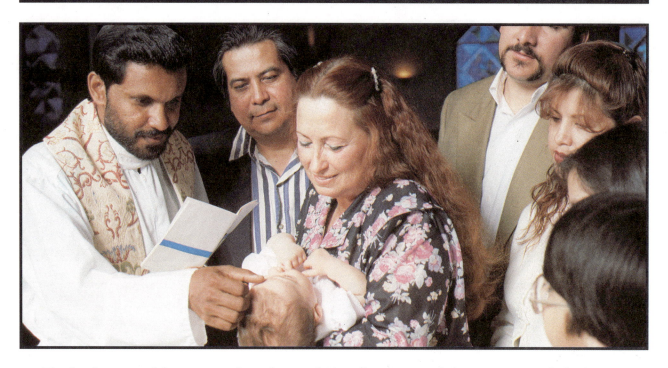

Each time we bless ourselves by making the Sign of the Cross with holy water at church, we are remembering our Baptism.

Each time we make the Sign of the Cross, we show we love Jesus and want to be part of his family.

The Church is more than a building.

The Church is a community of people who, by their Baptism, belong to the Family of God. Jesus is a very special person in this family. We Catholics believe that in Baptism our lives have been joined with Jesus' life and so he is present in a special way in the Catholic Church community.

We Belong

We Belong to God

Jesus the Good Shepherd calls me by name
_____.
(Name)

We Belong to Our Family

I belong to the _____ Family.

These people also belong to my family.

_____
_____
_____
_____
_____
_____
_____

We Belong to God's Church Family

At my Baptism, I became a member of the Catholic Church.

I belong to the _____ Parish Family.

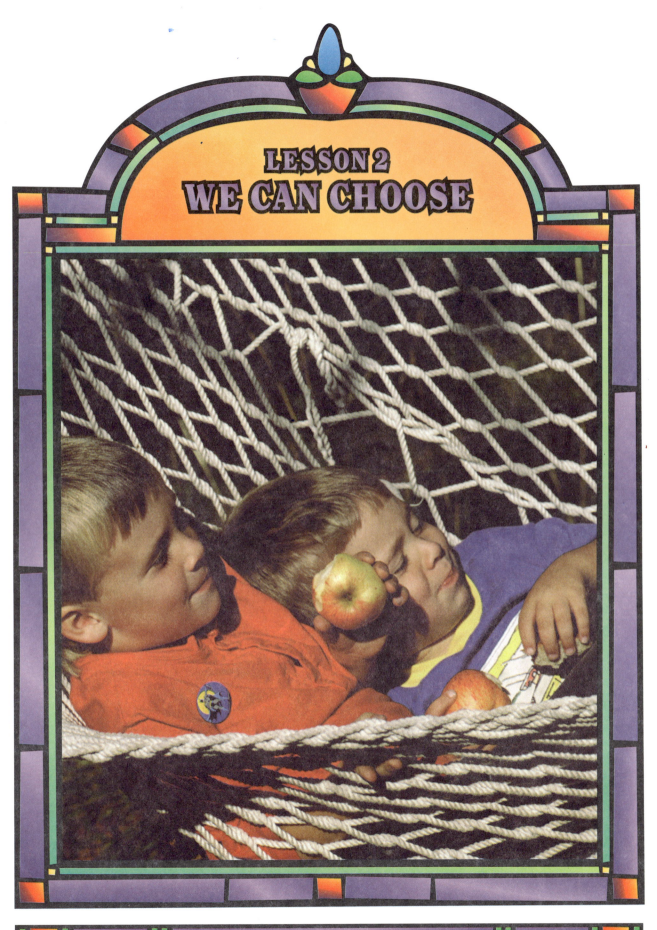

The Festival

Sandy and Ron were neighbors and friends. Both were eight years old. And both were looking forward to the parish festival, which was held every fall.

Sandy and Ron lived only a few blocks from St. Ann's. The day before the festival, they went to the church grounds to see the workers put up the tents and booths. They watched them set up the rides: a merry-go-round, a Ferris wheel, a tumble bug, and little cars that ran on tracks.

On the day of the festival, Sandy and Ron were up early. They could hardly wait until noon when the giant firecrackers would be set off. The firecrackers would tell everybody that the festival was beginning.

Sandy's mother gave her five dollars to spend. Ron had five dollars to spend, too. This was quite a lot because their families did not have much money.

As they walked over to the festival, Ron and Sandy talked about what they would do first. They went to the merry-go-round. Ron reached for his money to buy a ticket for a ride. His pocket was empty.

"My money's gone!" Ron exclaimed. "Now I can't go on any of the rides."

Sandy helped Ron look all over for the money. They retraced their steps. They didn't find it. Ron looked very sad.

Then Sandy said, "Ron, you can have half of my money. We can share. Then both of us can go on some rides."

The two rode on the merry-go-round and the Ferris wheel. They shared a cotton candy. And then the money was gone.

After that, Ron and Sandy watched other people on the rides until it was time to go home. Later that evening, Sandy told her mother and father what happened.

Her mother said, "It was nice of you to share your money with Ron."

"Yes," said her father, "that makes us very proud of you. I'm sure Ron appreciated it, too."

DOCTRINAL STORY

You Can Choose

The grown-ups in your family make many choices for you.

They tell you what time to get up and what time to go to bed.

They say things such as, "Do your homework now."

"Eat all your carrots."

"Be nice to your brother."

They tell you things you need to do to learn and grow.

Your family does not always choose for you. As you get older you make more choices for yourself. You learn how to use the wonderful gift that God has given only to people.

You are free to choose between right and wrong. Learning to choose well takes time and practice. Your family helps you learn to make good choices. Jesus helps you learn to make good choices too.

All his life, Jesus chose to love and help other people. He always chose what was good and right. This is what his heavenly Father wanted him to do. He taught people how much God loves them. He taught them to choose what is good and avoid what is wrong. He taught them to do this for the love of God.

Jesus has always loved us. He chose us to be part of his family. Sometimes we do not return that love. Sometimes we do not act as if we are part of his family. Sometimes we choose things that Jesus taught us are wrong.

When we do something on purpose that is against what Jesus or God, the Father, has taught us, we commit *sin*.

Sin always hurts our friendship

with God. Sin also takes away from the love in the Church.

But when we ask for forgiveness, we strengthen our friendship with God.

Jesus teaches us that God, our loving Father, is always ready to forgive and forget.

He offers us his forgiveness in the Sacrament of Penance/Reconciliation.

In this sacrament, the priest represents Jesus. He also represents all the people that belong to the Church family.

In this sacrament, we talk to the priest who is listening just as Jesus listens. The priest talks to us, prays with us, and guides us. When he forgives us, it is Jesus who forgives us. His power to forgive has been given to him by Jesus.

God loves us all so much that he never wants to be separated from us. The Sacrament of Penance/Reconciliation keeps us close together.

So, even when we choose to go against what Jesus wants, if we are sorry, Jesus welcomes us back.

THE RITE

Getting Ready for Reconciliation
I Examine My Conscience

I find a quiet place where I can think and pray.
I think about God's love for me.
I know that God wants me to be good.

I ask myself what choices I have made that have led me to do and say things that are wrong.

These are the sins I will talk to the priest about in my First Reconciliation.

IN THE LORD'S PEACE • LESSON 2

ACTIVITY PAGE

What Might Happen?

What might happen if you did any of these things? Draw a line to the words that tell.

1. If you choose to say hello to a new child in the neighborhood, you might . . .

2. If you choose to play on the way to school, you might . . .

3. If you choose to make fun of a neighbor, you might . . .

4. If you choose to play with your little brother or sister, you might . . .

5. If you choose to play in a field full of weeds, you might . . .

6. If you choose to play at a friend's house after school without asking, you might . . .

7. If you choose to hang up your clothes and put your toys away, you might . . .

8. If you choose to keep your dog's water bowl filled, you might . . .

- be late for class and get in trouble.
- hurt the person's feelings.
- get poison ivy.
- make a new friend.
- have fun yourself.
- have a healthy pet.
- worry someone.
- make someone's work easier.

IN THE LORD'S PEACE • LESSON 2   17

ACTIVITY PAGE

I Choose
My Favorite Things

Draw a picture or write the name of a favorite thing in each block.

a favorite color	a favorite dessert
a favorite friend	a favorite toy
a favorite place	a favorite animal

WORDS TO KNOW

Finish the letters in these words. Read the words aloud and tell what they mean.

A sign or symbol of God's love for us.

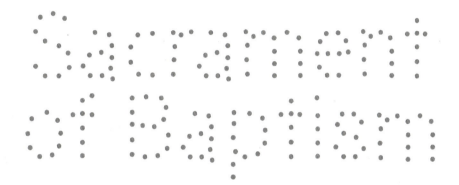

Through Baptism we become children of God free to grow in God's love.

God's spirit inside you calling you to be good and turn away from sin.

LET US PRAY

Dear God,
You have made a world full of so many good things.
You have made a world full of so many good people.
There are so many things to choose.
There are so many people to love.
Thank you for letting us choose.
Thank you for all of our favorite things and people.

FAMILY PAGE

This page is for you and your family to work on at home.

More Choosing

Some of the people in your family have already made some very important choices.

Ask each person to write his or her name in the first column, an important choice they have made in the second column, and in the third column why they made that important choice.

After finishing this **Family Page** pray together the prayer on p. 22.

Name	An important choice	Why that choice was made

FAMILY PRAYER

Loving Father,

You have made each person in our family special.

Some of the people in our family have already chosen their life's work. Some have chosen the person they want to share their life with. Some have chosen to be parents. In the years ahead, the rest of us will make these big and important choices. We will choose the work we will do. We may choose a husband or a wife or to live as a single person in the world. Or we may choose to be a priest or sister or brother. But, Lord, no matter what big choices we make, we will make other important choices each day, just as we do now. We will choose to accept your love or not. We will choose to help other people or not.

Lord, help us to choose wisely, to love you, and to help others always. Amen.

THEME

God loves us so much that he gives us the freedom to make choices.

GOALS

As a result of this lesson, you and your child should:

1. Experience through the family, the catechist, the priest, and others in the parish family God's special love for you.
2. Recognize that God made you to be like himself: loving and happy.
3. Be aware that you can and do make choices.
4. Be glad and thankful for the gift of choosing.
5. See some of the consequences of the choices that you make.
6. Be glad that God has given you Jesus to help you learn how to choose.
7. Recognize the sacraments as signs of God's love and know that when you celebrate the sacraments, Jesus gives you the special help you need for growing in God's love.
8. Know that penance is about celebrating God's love and forgiveness.
9. Look forward to celebrating the Sacrament of Penance for the first time.

MESSAGE

Writing, drawing, cutting, pasting, and other craft activities enable you to teach your child some basic ideas about God's saving love. These are: God created us because he loves us. He recreates us through Jesus. He loves us so much he does not want us to be destroyed by our sin and selfishness. Jesus, from the time of Baptism, shares our lives, binding himself to us so that we will not become slaves to our sin and selfishness. Of course, we are weak and we behave selfishly. If we let him, Jesus will keep us from losing ourselves to sin forever. He helps God's life — or grace — grow in us. In the Eucharist Jesus renews this freeing life that he won on the cross for us. In penance he helps us accept the saving love and forgiveness that God is always waiting to give us when we have chosen to sin or to behave selfishly.

Allen's Bad Day

Allen Thomas was pouring himself a glass of milk for breakfast. It was Saturday. Allen always fixed his own breakfast on Saturday. His mother slept in a little later.

Allen had the glass almost full. Then the milk carton slipped put of his hand. The carton fell on the glass. The glass fell to the floor and broke with a loud crash. Milk and broken glass were everywhere.

Mrs. Thomas woke up and hurried into the kitchen. She was happy to see that Allen was all right. But she was angry when she saw the mess.

The spilled milk and broken glass were soon cleaned up. Allen and his mother ate breakfast together. They both felt better.

Later that morning, Allen was playing with his dog, Flash, in the back yard. Allen's friend David came walking up the street. Allen opened the gate to talk to him. While they were talking, Flash ran through the gate and out of the yard.

Allen, Mrs. Thomas, and David spent the next hour looking for Flash. They finally found the dog in a nearby woods. He was covered with burrs. Allen and his mother worked for an hour on Flash's coat.

That afternoon, Allen's grandmother phoned. She had planned to take Allen to a movie. She told him she had twisted her foot so they wouldn't be able to go that day. They could go sometime next week.

Allen felt that the whole day was ruined. Nothing was going right.

Allen's mother asked him to pick up his games and toys. Allen didn't pick them up. Finally Mrs. Thomas made Allen sit down and think about his actions. After some time Allen decided to pick up his games and toys.

When bedtime came, Allen asked his mother to read a story with him. When they were finished he asked, "Aren't you mad at me, Mom?"

"No," she said, "why should I be mad at you?"

"I broke the glass, and let the dog get loose. Then I didn't pick up my stuff."

"I love you all the time," said Mrs. Thomas. "I get a little upset about accidents, like the milk. I get upset when Flash gets loose. And I don't like it when you leave your games out and don't pick them up. But I never stop loving you. I think all mothers and fathers get upset just because they do love their children. Now let's get ready to go to sleep."

Allen and Mrs. Thomas prayed together. When prayers were finished, Mrs. Thomas gave Allen a kiss and turned out the light. He went to sleep peacefully.

DOCTRINAL STORY

The Loving Father

Once there was a man who owned a big farm. It was so big that he needed many workers to take care of the land and animals.

The man had two sons.

He loved his sons dearly.

"Someday," he said, "I will give each of you a piece of land for your own."

But the younger son did not want to wait for someday.

"I want my land now," he said.

So the father gave each son some land.

The older son chose to stay at home. He helped his father with the farm.

The younger son sold his land right away. He took the money and went to a far-off country to have a good time.

He spent and spent and spent.

He did many wrong things.

Soon he did not even have a penny.

Then hard times came to that far-off country. The poor were starving.

The young man could find only a job feeding pigs.

The son was hungry enough to eat the pigs' food. But the man who owned the pigs would not even let him do that.

The starving son thought about his father.

"What a wonderful father I have. He is so good and kind. I am not good enough to be his son. But I will go home and ask for a job on the farm."

All the time the son was gone, his father thought about him. He wondered if his son was well and happy. He missed him very much. He hoped that his son would soon come home again.

Every day he went out to the road. He hoped that he would see his son walking home.

At last one day the father saw his son. He was so happy. He ran to meet him. He hugged his son and kissed him.

"I have sinned," said the son. "I am no longer fit to be your son."

But the father loved his son so much, he forgave him for everything he had done. And he gave a grand party to celebrate his son's return.

Jesus told this story about the loving father. He tells us that God is like the loving father in the story. He is always ready to forgive.

THE RITE

The Greeting
I Meet the Priest

I go to the reconciliation room. The priest welcomes me and helps me to feel good about coming.

I tell the priest that this is my First Reconciliation.

The priest and I make the Sign of the Cross saying,

"In the name of the Father, and of the Son, and of the Holy Spirit. Amen."

IN THE LORD'S PEACE • LESSON 3

ACTIVITY PAGE

Tell About the Loving Father

In each picture, the father is thinking about his lost son. Finish the father's words in each picture.

I wonder how my son is. I think of him _____

If I saw my son, I would feel _____

I wonder if he has enough of the things he needs. He needs _____

I wonder if he has forgotten me. That would make me feel _____

IN THE LORD'S PEACE • LESSON 3

ACTIVITY PAGE

God is like the loving father in this story. God wants only good for us.

He never stops loving us, even when we do wrong things.

He is always waiting for us to say, "I am sorry."

He is always ready to say, "I forgive you. Come home to me."

God, our loving Father, forgives and forgets.

WORDS TO KNOW

Finish the letters in these words. Read the words aloud and tell what they mean.

forgive

You do this when you love a person who has hurt you, and you make up.

the priest

The person who acts for Jesus and the Church in the Sacrament of Penance.

LET US PRAY

Leader: Who is like the father in the story of the loving father?

All: God is.

Leader: Who is like the runaway son?

All: We all are sometimes.

Leader: Dear Father,
We are sorry that we sometimes forget how much you love us.
But we are glad that you never stop loving us.
We are glad that you chose us to be your children.
Help us to choose what is good.
Thank you for giving us Jesus for our brother and good friend.
Thank you for the love and forgiveness you give us.
Soon we will celebrate your love and forgiveness in the Sacrament of Penance for the first time.
Please help us to get ready.
We make our prayer in the name of Jesus, who is with us in the Spirit.

All: Amen.

FAMILY PAGE

This page is for you to work on at home with your family.

The Son Who Returned

You know the story of the loving father and the runaway son. Tell the story to your family. Then draw a picture of the father welcoming his son home. You draw the father and son. Ask your family to draw the other parts of the picture. They can put in the house, the road, trees, and anything else they like.

FAMILY PRAYER

Response: Father, we thank you.

Leader: Let us thank God, our Father, for all the love he gives this family.

For the gift of each other, (R).

For being with us in our happy times, (R).

For being with us in our troubled times, (R).

Sometimes we forget how much you love us, and we are sorry for that.

But you never stop loving us, and we are glad for that.

Thank you for giving us Jesus to be our brother and good friend.

Thank you for the love and forgiveness you give us every day.

Thank you for the love and forgiveness you give us in the Sacrament of Penance. We pray in Jesus' name.

All: Amen.

Leader: Let us pray the special prayer Jesus taught us. (Turn to p. 95.)

Leader: Let us share with one another a sign of peace.

THEME

God never stops loving us, even when we sin. He understands our weakness and is glad to forgive us if we accept his love and forgiveness.

GOALS

As a result of this lesson, you and your child should:

1. Know that God always loves you.
2. Understand that when you do selfish, unloving things, you turn away from God's love; God does not turn away from you.
3. Know that no matter how bad the things may be that you do, God keeps on loving you, offering you his forgiveness. You have only to turn back and receive the love and forgiveness God wants to give.
4. Feel that you need never be afraid to ask God's forgiveness.
5. Understand that God is always glad to forgive you when you are sorry.

MESSAGE

The parable of the prodigal son is used to teach the children that God never stops loving us, no matter how sinful we may be. We have only to do as the runaway son did — turn back to God to accept all the love and forgiveness that has been there for us all along. The Sacrament of Penance is a celebration of our return to our loving and forgiving Father in heaven.

Allison and the Canoe

Allison played at Mary Beth's house all the time. The two girls were in the same class in school. They usually walked to school together.

Mary Beth had an older brother, Ben. Ben had an entire toy village in his room. There were tepees, horses, and even canoes just like those used by Native Americans long ago.

Ben let Allison and Mary Beth play with his village. Allison especially enjoyed it. She was starting to build a village of her own at home.

One day Allison and Mary Beth were playing with Ben's village. They pretended they were different tribes as they moved the little toy people around the camp.

As they were playing, Mary Beth had to leave the room to answer the telephone. While Mary Beth was gone, Allison picked up one of the three canoes. It was the prettiest one because it had symbols and figures painted on its sides. Ben liked it best of all, too.

Allison began to think how nice the canoe would look in her village. She thought about it. She could hide it in her room and play with it by herself. She could put it in her coat pocket now. That way, no one would know she took it.

Ben would be sad to lose it. He might think one of his friends took it.

Allison chose. She took the canoe, even though she knew it was wrong. She put it in her coat pocket.

When Mary Beth came back, Allison said it was time to go home. She put on her coat and left.

At home, Allison took out the canoe. She loved it. It looked just right as part of her village. Then she hid it so her mother wouldn't see it.

Allison could not stop thinking about what she had done. She knew Ben would be upset about the missing canoe. She knew his whole family would be upset, too. Allison felt very sad about what she did. She was sad and afraid. What would she do?

Later that afternoon, Allison went back to Mary Beth's home. She had the canoe in her coat pocket. When she saw her chance, she put the canoe back in Ben's village. Then she felt a lot better.

DOCTRINAL STORY

Jesus Helps Sinners

God loves us.

God knows we are happiest when we love him and when we love others.

God gave us a set of rules to help us be happy.

These rules tell us what we must do to love God and others.

These rules about love are called the *commandments*.

God sent his Son, Jesus, to us.

Jesus showed us how to live these commandments:

> Jesus loved his Father, God, and honored him above all things.
> He prayed to God every day.
> Jesus kept God's special day, the Sabbath, holy.
> Jesus loved all people and hurt no one. He said kind things.
> He helped people.
> Jesus loved and obeyed his parents.
> Jesus never took what did not belong to him.
> Jesus always told the truth.
> Jesus was never jealous.
> Jesus preached about how important it is for mothers and fathers to love and respect each other.

One time Jesus said that a certain two commandments were the most important.

He said that if we keep these two, we will keep all the rest.

The first one is:
"You shall love the Lord, your God, with all your heart, with all your soul, and with all your mind."

The second one is:
"You shall love your neighbor as yourself" (Matthew 22:37-39).

Sometimes it is hard to love.
We say mean things.
We do mean things.
Sometimes we do and say these things on purpose.
We hurt people.
When we do and say mean things on purpose, we sin.
But even then, God does not stop loving us.
God does not say, "Go away, you sinner. I don't want anything to do with you."
God reaches out to us with love and forgives us.
God wants to help us to do better.
God helps us find forgiveness.

We pray to God and tell God we are sorry.
We tell the people we have hurt that we are sorry.
We ask them to forgive us.
We go to the Sacrament of Penance/Reconciliation.

We accept Jesus' love and ask his forgiveness.

Jesus never sinned.
But he did not turn away from sinners. Jesus came into the world to help them.
The Bible tells of many different sinners Jesus helped.
Jesus forgave sinners and healed them.
Jesus helped them to accept God's love and forgiveness.
Jesus died on a cross to save us.

Jesus rose to a new life.

Jesus is with us every day.
Jesus is with us at special times, too.
Jesus first came to us in Baptism.
There, he became our brother and good friend, and he made us part of God's family.
Jesus also comes to us in the

Sacrament of Penance/Reconciliation to heal us and forgive us through the priest.

But, most of all, of course, he is with us in *Holy Communion*.

There, he is present — as our loving God, our Savior, our source of life.

Now, if we let him, he can overcome sin in our lives.

He can help us.

Jesus can heal us.

THE RITE

Reading the Word of God
I Hear the Words of Jesus

The priest and I read together from the Bible.

We read how God is always ready to forgive.

We read about how much Jesus loves us.

Jesus said, "Let the children come to me, and do not prevent them; for the kingdom of heaven belongs to such as these." After he placed his hands on them, he went away.
          Matthew 19:14-15

Try to think of times when you turned to Jesus for help. Then complete the following:

I asked Jesus for help once when it was really important. I can remember the exact spot where I was:

_____

_____

ACTIVITY PAGE

The Paper-Bag Plays

Find small lunch bags and crayons.
Draw faces on the bags.
Make them look like the people in the short plays on this and the following pages.

You and a friend can say the words.
Put your hands inside the paper bags.
Move the bags when you say the words.
The paper-bag puppets will look as if they are talking.

A person in each play will make a mistake,
have an accident, or sin.
You should decide which you think the person has done.

Blast Off

Susan: Let's pretend my bed is a spaceship. We're flying to a new planet.

Rosa: Okay! Start the engine. Roar!

Susan: Blast off. Zoom!

Rosa: All rockets are working.

Susan: Zoom! Zoom! Zoom! We're almost there!

Mother: You children are making too much noise. You woke up the baby.

Check one answer.

Susan and Rosa have:
☐ had an accident.
☐ sinned.
☐ made a mistake.

ACTIVITY PAGE

Karen and the Tulips

Mrs. Simmons: Karen, please don't run through my yard. I'm afraid my tulips will get hurt.

Karen: Yes, Mrs. Simmons. (Mrs. Simmons leaves.) That crab. I'm going to get even with her. I'll make her feel bad. I'll break off all of her old flowers. (Karen jumps on the tulips. Karen leaves.)

Mrs. Simmons: (She comes out of her house.) Oh, my goodness! All my beautiful tulips are broken. (She cries as she goes back into the house.)

Check one answer.

Karen has:
❏ had an accident.
❏ sinned.
❏ made a mistake.

Jimmy and the Math Problem

Teacher: Jimmy, can you add four and five?

Jimmy: Is it seven?

Teacher: No. Let me show you how to add these numbers.

Check one answer.

Jimmy has:
❏ had an accident.
❏ sinned.
❏ made a mistake.

You Decide

Only one person in all the plays sinned, the person who wanted to hurt someone. The person knew he or she was doing something wrong. This person thought about the action. This person chose to do the action. This person's name is _____.

Remember this: We all have accidents and make mistakes. Jesus does not want us to think we are bad because of them. We did not mean to hurt anyone.

Sometimes we do bad things on purpose. We hurt people on purpose. Then we should feel sorrowful and guilty. These bad things are called _____.

Remember this too: Jesus loves us all the time. He loves us even when we sin. He wants us to be his friends. And finally, Jesus teaches us not to judge or make fun of people who do wrong things. We need to correct our own faults. We need to be forgiving just like Jesus.

WORDS TO KNOW

Finish the letters in these words. Read the words aloud and tell what they mean.

This is another word for forgive.

Something you do on purpose that goes against God's law.

True sorrow for sin. We have this when we tell God we are sorry.

LET US PRAY

Dear Jesus,
We know that God wants us to love others.
We say and do many kind things.
We make others happy.

It is hard to be kind all the time.
It is hard not to be selfish.
Sometimes we sin.
We say mean things on purpose.
We do mean things on purpose.
We hurt people.
We make them unhappy.

Jesus, please help us to do better.
We know you are with us every day.
You are willing to help us if we ask.
We will try to remember to ask for your help every day.

Soon, Jesus, you will be with us in a new way.
You will be with us in the Sacrament of Penance.
We are glad that you are going to give us this new help.

FAMILY PAGE

This page is for you to work on at home with your family.

Make a Fish Mobile

When we sin, we say no to God's love. We say no to Jesus. We do things God doesn't want us to do. This mobile will help you remember to do things Jesus wants you to do. It will remind you to say yes to Jesus.

The fish is a sign used by Jesus' followers. Some of his early followers spoke Greek. The letters in the Greek word for fish reminded Christians that Jesus was God's Son and our Savior. So they drew the simple picture of a fish as a sign that they followed Jesus. It was like a secret code. If you look around your church, you might see a fish sign. It is a sign of Jesus.

Make the mobile you see on this page. It will be a sign that Jesus' life and love are with you. Ask someone at home to help you trace the pattern onto a sheet of paper. Trace two patterns for each fish. Cut out the pieces and draw their outline on cardboard. Color the paper fish.

Cut out the cardboard pieces. Paste the colored fish onto the cardboard pieces, one on each side. Make holes where they are shown. Hang the pieces of the mobile from a stick with thread. Hang the mobile in your room.

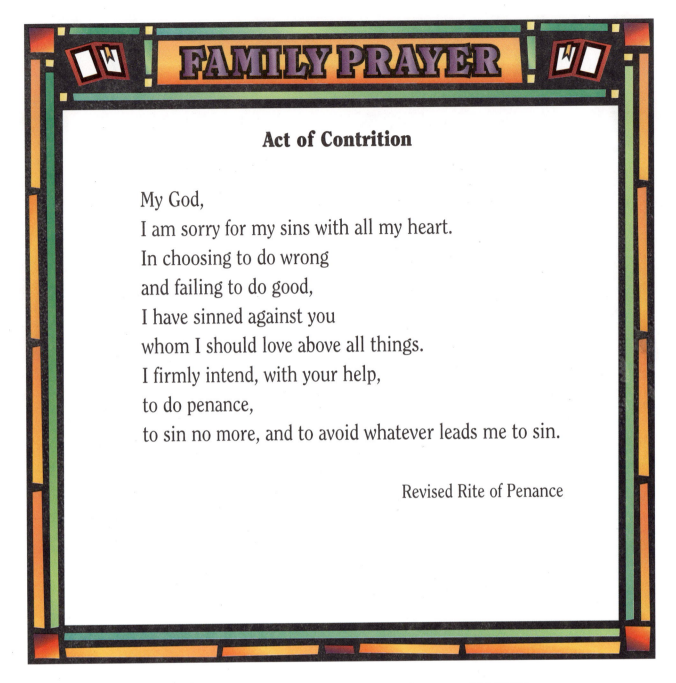

FAMILY PRAYER

Act of Contrition

My God,
I am sorry for my sins with all my heart.
In choosing to do wrong
and failing to do good,
I have sinned against you
whom I should love above all things.
I firmly intend, with your help,
to do penance,
to sin no more, and to avoid whatever leads me to sin.

Revised Rite of Penance

THEME
Sin is a deliberate refusal to do what we know God wants.

GOALS
As a result of this lesson, you and your child should:
1. Know that mistakes and accidents are not sins.
2. Know that sin is deliberately choosing to do something you know is unloving.
3. Understand that sin always hurts the sinner and his or her relationship with God, and takes away from the love in God's family.
4. Understand that we are all sinners but that God sent Jesus to help us become more loving persons, freed from sin.
5. Know that God gave his family the commandments because he loves us and wants us to be happy.
6. See the commandments as rules in God's family that help us live in peace.

MESSAGE
We have the power to choose — and sometimes we choose to sin. This lesson teaches the conditions that make a thought or act sinful. It also presents the Ten Commandments and the two "great" commandments as laws that help us be happy because they tell us what we must do to love God and others. That is the way to true happiness. Additional help in distinguishing between sin, accidents, and mistakes is given the child in this lesson.

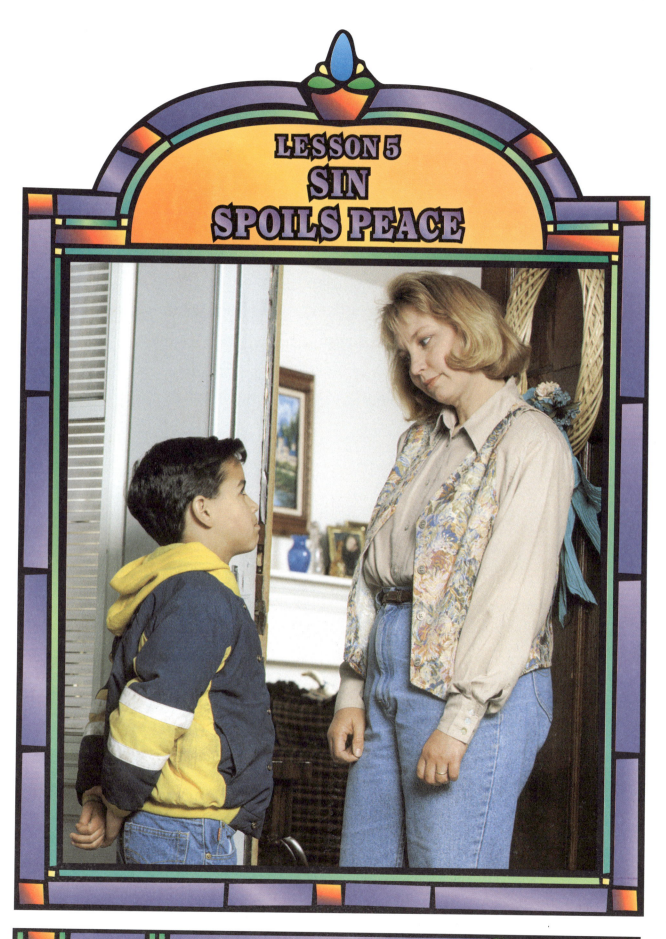

Best Friends

Jerry and Don had been best friends since before kindergarten. They played together almost every day. On rainy days or sunny days, Don and Jerry could usually be found together.

In the early summer, a new family moved into the neighborhood. They had three children.

"I wonder if there are any kids our age?" Don asked Jerry.

They watched the moving van pull away. Just then, a boy in jeans and a t-shirt came walking around the side of the new family's house.

"Hey great!" said Jerry. "Let's go meet him."

Don went up to the new boy first. "Hi, I'm Don, and this is my friend Jerry. You movin' in here?"

In only a few minutes, Don and Jerry knew that the new boy would be a lot of fun. His name was Matt.

The boys sat under a tree and talked about school and baseball. Matt asked them to come to his backyard to hit a softball. Jerry didn't like softball very much, but he thought he'd play anyway.

Don was a good ball player. Soon, anyone could see that Matt was very good, too.

After only fifteen minutes, Jerry sat down on the back porch.

He watched as Don and Matt threw flies and grounders to each other.

"Let's go over to my house and play," Jerry said.

"Naw," said Don. "This is fun. Come on."

Jerry was quiet.

In a few more minutes Jerry called again, "Let's ride bikes."

"Mine's still packed up," said Matt.

Jerry stood up and began to walk around the house. He and Don had always done things together. Now with Matt here, would he lose his best friend? He was starting to feel sad.

As he walked down the family's driveway, he kicked at the stones. A big one flew up and hit the car that was parked there. Jerry didn't pay much attention.

When he got home, he ate lunch and then went to his room. All afternoon he moped around.

"I've lost my best friend," he thought.

Once he thought he heard Don and Matt playing in Matt's front yard. He got even sadder.

That night, Jerry's mom asked him if he'd met the new kids across the street.

"One of them," said Jerry.

"Is he nice?" his mom asked.

"He's all right, I guess," was Jerry's answer.

By this time, he was angry at Matt for taking away his best friend.

After supper the doorbell rang as usual. It was Don.

"Let's go!" he said to Jerry.

"Is Matt coming?" Jerry asked.

Don said, "He can't come out for a week. He's in trouble. His father thinks he dented their new car when we were playing in the front yard. He can't play out with anybody."

Jerry thought about the stone he had kicked when he was leaving the yard. "That wasn't . . ." Jerry began to say. But then he thought to himself, "If Matt's grounded, Don will play with me."

"What did you say?" Don asked.

"Oh, nothin'! It's too bad," was Jerry's reply.

Don and Jerry got on their bikes and rode off. It wasn't long before Jerry began to feel bad. He knew being quiet was like lying, and he knew lying was wrong.

That night he didn't sleep well. The next morning, Jerry and Don dragged out some old wood to build a fort near Don's garage.

Don said, "You know I didn't see Matt hit that car with anything. Boy, was his dad mad."

Jerry was quiet. Soon he got on his bike to go home for lunch. As he rode by Matt's house, he turned suddenly into Matt's yard. Shaking a little, he walked to the door and knocked. A lady answered. She was wearing cleaning clothes.

"Are you Matt's mom?" asked Jerry.

"Yes," the lady said.

At first, Jerry could say nothing. Then the words just seemed to pour out. "Matt didn't dent the car. I did. I was kicking stones in the driveway. One flew up and hit the car. I was mad and didn't . . ."

Matt's mother smiled, "What's your name?" "Jerry Wills," Jerry said. Then Matt's mother invited Jerry in and called Matt out of his room. Matt and Jerry shook hands. And Matt asked if Jerry could stay for lunch.

"Certainly," Matt's mom said.

Everything was better. That night Jerry slept peacefully.

ACTIVITY PAGE

The Road to Peace

Below you see the road to peace. Follow it. Color the road to peace with your favorite color. Be careful of the wrong turns. They will keep you from finding peace. Begin at the bottom of the page where it says START HERE.

Imagine you start a fight with a friend. You and your friend are angry. The people who play with you and your friend are upset. They want you and your friend to be happy again. How can you find peace again?

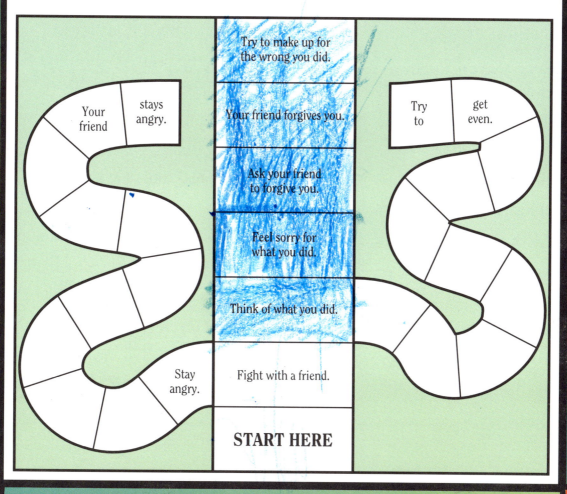

IN THE LORD'S PEACE • LESSON 5

A Happy Family

In a happy family, everyone helps.
Everybody says kind things.
Everybody is thoughtful.
Nobody feels mean or jealous.
The family has fun working and playing and just being together.
The house is full of good feelings.

No family is like that all the time.
Sometimes people get tired and grumpy.
They feel sick.
They have accidents. They make mistakes.
Feelings get hurt.
People are upset.
But still, there is love in the family.

Other times, one person may do something mean and nasty to another family member.
These two people are angry with each other then.
Maybe they stop speaking.
But they are not the only ones who get hurt.
Everybody in the family feels bad about what has happened.
It is hard to be happy when somebody in the family is unhappy.
No one is really happy again until the angry people make up.
Then the house is full of good feelings again.
The family is glad when there is peace again.
They feel like celebrating.

A **saint** named Paul had a good rule to help happy families stay happy.
He said we should never let the sun go down on our anger.
Paul meant that each day of our lives should end peacefully.

The words of Jesus help us to find happiness and peace in our families too. Jesus gave us the secret of being happy.

When Jesus saw the crowds he went up to the mountainside. After he had sat down, his disciples gathered around him, and he began to teach them:

> Happy are the people who care more about God and other people than they do money and owning lots of things.
>
> Happy are the people who know that their sadness and sorrow will pass and look forward to perfect joy with God.
>
> Happy are the unimportant people who know they are important in God's eyes.
>
> Happy are the people who want more than anything to be good. They shall have their prayers answered.
>
> Happy are the people who forgive others. God will forgive them.
>
> Happy are the people who think only of doing what is right. They are sure to see God.
>
> Happy are the people with kind and peaceful hearts. They are true children of God.
>
> Happy are the people who are mistreated because they want to do what is right. God will give them his kingdom.
>
> Happy are the people who are mistreated because they love and follow Jesus. Their reward in heaven shall be great.
>
> from Matthew 5:1-12

THE RITE

Confession of Sins
I Talk With the Priest

I tell the priest how I have acted selfishly and hurt others.

I confess my sins.

The priest asks me if I did these things on purpose.

The priest wants to find out if the things I tell him about are really sins.

Accepting a Penance
I Will Try to Do Better

The priest helps me to be sorry for my sins.

I tell the priest that I will try to do better.

The priest gives me something to do, an act of kindness and some special prayers to help me be more loving.

The acts of kindness and the special prayers are called a penance.

ACTIVITY PAGE

Sacrament of Penance/Reconciliation

Soon you will celebrate the Sacrament of Penance/Reconciliation. This sacrament offers God's forgiveness and peace.

It is also a sign that you are at peace with others. The priest, acting for the whole Church, brings God's peace in the Sacrament of Penance. A big word for living at peace is "reconciliation."

Circle the words that you think lead to reconciliation.

sorry

love

peace

insult

pout

fight

lie

forgive

anger

IN THE LORD'S PEACE • LESSON 5

WORDS TO KNOW

Finish the letters in these words. Read the words aloud and tell what they mean.

God's big family. When we sin, we hurt the Church. When we do good, we help God's big family and build peace.

To tell your sins to the priest.

WORDS TO KNOW

peace

The feeling inside that comes when you love God and others.

penance

The name of the sacrament of forgiveness. Something the priest gives you to show you are sorry for your sins. It can be a prayer or good deed.

LET US PRAY

Dear God,

We are sorry for all our sins.

We feel bad because our sins hurt us.

We feel bad because our sins hurt one another.

They spoil the love and peace in our family.

Most of all, we feel sorry because we said no to your love.

We feel very bad because we said no to someone who loves us so much.

Help us to stay on the road of love and peace.

Help us remember the words of St. Paul and never let the sun go down on our anger.

We pray in Jesus' name. Amen.

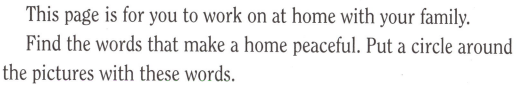

This page is for you to work on at home with your family.

Find the words that make a home peaceful. Put a circle around the pictures with these words.

FAMILY PRAYER

Response: We're building God's peace.

Leader: Dear God, bless this family. Bless _____ (names of family members). Help us to love one another as you love us. Help us to say yes to what you want. Help us to live in peace and love.

When we help one another, (R).
When we care about one another's feelings, (R).
When we share what we have, (R).
When we love the truth, (R).
When we are glad for each other, (R).
When we take the blame for what we did, (R).
When we say, "I'm sorry," (R).
When we say, "I forgive you," (R).
When we try to make up for hurting each other, (R).
Let us give one another a sign of peace. Amen.

THEME

Sin makes it difficult for friends and families to get along and to be happy; it hurts the sinner and the people directly or indirectly concerned; it diminishes the love in God's family, the Church.

GOALS

As a result of this lesson, you and your child should:

1. Understand that we are all sinners and in need of forgiveness.
2. Understand that when we sin, we hurt ourselves and others and do not give to God the love he deserves.
3. Realize that sin diminishes the love in God's family, the Church.
4. Be more aware of attitudes and actions that spoil peace.
5. Know that we are not really sorry for hurting others unless we ask forgiveness and try to make up for the hurt.
6. Realize that when we hurt someone, even though it may not be a sin, we need to make up for the hurt.
7. Understand that there is no peace until we are truly sorry for the wrong done, ask forgiveness of the person or persons hurt, ask forgiveness of God, and do something loving to help make up for the hurt.

MESSAGE

Love and forgiveness are essential to happiness in our family at home, in God's family, the Church, and in the entire human family. This lesson deals with the communal nature of sin and reconciliation. Sin hurts not only the person offended, but also the sinner and the other people who share their lives. Saying "I'm sorry" and "I forgive you" is usually not easy, but both are essential in restoring peace.

Lynn Talks Back

Lynn thought she must be a bad person. She always seemed to talk back. She talked back to her father. She talked back to her grandmother. Once in a while, she even talked back to her teacher. Lynn talked back all the time.

Her mother kept telling her that talking back was rude. And afterward, Lynn was always sorry. She told the people she talked back to she was sorry. She told Jesus she was sorry.

Still, Lynn worried. Was she really a bad person? Would people stop liking her because she talked back?

One day Lynn said to her grandmother, "Am I a bad person, Grandma?"

Grandma said, "Why do you think you're a bad person?"

"Because I always talk back," Lynn answered.

Grandma said, "That's your conscience telling you to try to be better. Are you sorry for the things you say?" Lynn nodded her head yes. "And do you say you are sorry?" Lynn nodded. "And do you try not to talk back?"

Lynn said, "Yes I really do. Sometimes I don't talk back when I want to. Then sometimes I do it again."

Grandmother said, "Lynn, I'm sure you are not a bad person. You do some bad things sometimes. But if you try not to do them and if you are sorry when you do them — well, that shows what kind of person you are."

"Look at all the good things you do," Grandmother said. "You help your mother don't you? You play nicely with your little sister. You try to get along with your friends."

"Yes, I try to do all those things," said Lynn.

Grandmother said, "Then stop worrying. Jesus loves you. If you ask him, he will always forgive you. That should make you feel better. And if you ask for his help, Jesus will help you to be better. You are a good person. And Jesus will help you get better and better."

ACTIVITY PAGE

1. Think quietly about something bad that you do over and over again. Are you sorry? What things do you do that show you are really sorry?

Sa _____

_____

_____

_____

_____

_____

2. Think quietly about good things you do. Make a list of them here.

_____

_____

_____

_____

_____

_____

_____

_____

ACTIVITY PAGE

3. Are you a good person? How does Jesus help you to be a good person? Name some good things that people say about you. Name some people who help you to be better and better.

_____
_____
_____
_____
_____
_____
_____
_____
_____
_____
_____
_____
_____
_____
_____
_____

DOCTRINAL STORY

Peter Sins

Peter was one of the first people to follow Jesus. He was an Apostle. He was a very good man. He loved God. He loved Jesus.

Jesus picked Peter to be the first leader of his Church.

Jesus told all the Apostles that he, himself, would soon be arrested. He said when that happened, they would all run away. Even Peter would fail him.

Peter did not believe that he could do such a terrible thing to Jesus.

"No," he said, "the others may leave you, but I will always stay with you."

That very night Jesus was arrested. Peter was so afraid. He didn't keep his promise. He told people that he didn't even know Jesus.

Deep inside Peter felt ashamed. He knew that he had done a terrible thing.

"I do not deserve forgiveness," he told himself.

But he remembered what Jesus told him about God's love.

He knew that God had not stopped loving him.

He knew that he should not give up on himself.

God would help him to be a better person.

Peter was sorry that he had pretended not to know Jesus, his friend.

Peter was so sorry, he cried.

We are all something like Peter. We are good people. But we are weak too. Sometimes we sin.

Like Peter, we should not give up.

If we are sorry for our sins, God will take us back. His love will help us grow stronger.

God, our Father, gives us Jesus in the Sacrament of Penance/Reconciliation to help us find our way back to God.

We are all something like Peter.

We are good people.
But we are weak too.
Sometimes we sin.
Like Peter, we should not give up.
If we are sorry for our sins, God will take us back.

His love will help us grow stronger.
God, our Father, gives us Jesus in the Sacrament of Penance/Reconciliation to help us find our way back to God.

THE RITE

Prayer of the Penitent
I Say "I'm Sorry"

I tell God I am sorry.

I say an Act of Contrition.

By this prayer I ask God's forgiveness.

I also ask for Jesus' help to always follow his ways and walk in his light.

Receiving Absolution
I Receive Forgiveness

The priest forgives and blesses me in God's name.

He places his hands over my head and says, "I absolve you from your sins in the name of the Father, and of the Son, and of the Holy Spirit."

I answer, "Amen."

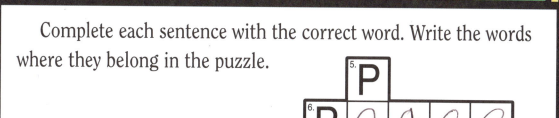

Complete each sentence with the correct word. Write the words where they belong in the puzzle.

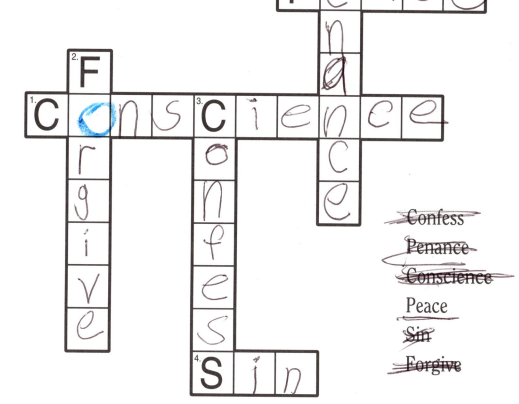

1. My _____ helps me tell the difference between what is good and what is wrong.
2. God will _____ me if I am really sorry.
3. I _____ my sins to the priest in reconciliation.
4. When I choose to _____ I turn away from God's love.
5. _____ will help me to be more loving.
6. _____ is feeling good in your heart.

WORDS TO KNOW

Finish the letters in these words. Read the words aloud and tell what they mean.

The words that the priest says to show that God has forgiven your sins.

This word means becoming friends once more.

LET US PRAY

Leader: When we don't pay attention to Jesus,
when we do not pray,
when we do not thank you for your love,
when we do not share your love with others,
Lord, have mercy.

All: Lord, have mercy.

Leader: You have given us people to guide us.
When we talk back to them,
when we disobey them,
Christ, have mercy.

All: Christ, have mercy.

Leader: When we fight with brothers and sisters and friends,
when we are slow to forgive others,
Lord, have mercy.

All: Lord, have mercy.

LET US PRAY

Leader: When we act selfishly, when we don't share things with others,
Christ, have mercy.

All: Christ, have mercy.

Leader: When we tell lies and blame others for our own faults,
Lord, have mercy.

All: Lord, have mercy.

Leader: When we act lazy, when we don't help at home or at school,
Christ, have mercy.

All: Christ, have mercy.

Leader: We have many chances to do good. Sometimes we fail.
Lord, have mercy.

All: Lord, have mercy.

FAMILY PAGE

This page is for you and your family to work on at home.

Reconciliation Brings Peace

Since our Baptism, we have not always done what is good. We do not always live as God wants us to. We do things that create problems for our family and friends. The Sacrament of Penance/Reconciliation makes us one big family again. Reconciliation restores peace. These people are a sign of God's family, the Church.

Draw arms to show their hands joined in one big family. Draw faces and hair. It might be fun to give them outfits.

FAMILY PRAYER

Response: Father, forgive us.

Leader: Father, you give us this family. You give us each other to love. But we are not always loving.

Someone wants a hug, and we hold it back, (R).

Someone wants us to listen, and we close our ears, (R).

Someone wants us to talk, and we are silent, (R).

Someone needs quiet, and we are noisy, (R).

Someone wants us to share, and we are selfish, (R).

Someone wants our forgiveness, and we say no, (R).

Someone wants the truth, and we tell lies, (R).

Someone gets more than we do, and we are jealous, (R).

Someone hurts us, and we get even, (R).

Someone says no to what we want, and we pout, (R).

All: Father, for our sins, we are sorry. Help us to forgive one another as you forgive us. Reconcile us. Help us to be more loving and peaceful. Amen.

THEME

Jesus teaches us that God never gives up on us, so we should never give up on ourselves.

GOALS

As a result of this lesson, you and your child should:

1. Be assured that God will never give up on you and is always ready to help.

2. Realize that no matter how many times you sin or how bad the sin may seem, God loves and forgives you.

3. Realize that you are basically good.

4. Understand that you need the love and forgiveness God offers to grow in love of God and others.

5. Make asking Jesus for forgiveness part of your daily prayer.

6. Know how to prepare for Reconciliation, what to say and do, and the importance of performing the penance afterwards.

MESSAGE

Photos, text, and activities present clear instruction to help your child learn how to prepare for Reconciliation, what to say and do, what to expect the priest to say and do, and what to do after Reconciliation.

This lesson admits that the road to peace is not easy. Bad habits can be tough to break. Strong temptations and emotions can lead us to sin. The child is reassured that Jesus is always ready to help. If we respond to his love and keep trying, we can find peace again.

Fran's First Reconciliation

Fran woke up excited on the day of her First Reconciliation. She knew that her parish family was going to share this special day in a penance celebration.

Fran's family and the families of the other children in her class would gather in the church. Father Smith, the pastor, would lead the parish in both asking and thanking God for his forgiveness.

Fran knew that when it came time for Reconciliation, her friend Father Martin, the assistant pastor, would be in the reconciliation room.

Father Martin had come to Fran's class three times to help prepare the children for their First Reconciliation. He would pray with her for the Lord's forgiveness.

At three o'clock that afternoon, Fran and her family went to the church. The pastor welcomed all the families.

"We are here to celebrate a great event today," he said. "Some children in our parish family will be receiving the Sacrament of Reconciliation for the first time. Let us share in their joy as they join us in building up the love and peace in our parish family."

Father Smith read some words of Jesus from the Bible. He led the people in prayer and song.

Fran felt very proud and grown up to be part of this important celebration.

Finally, Father Smith invited Fran and the other children to come to Reconciliation.

Fran sat quietly outside the reconciliation room waiting for her turn. She remembered her sins. She tried to remember why she had committed them. She talked to Jesus about them. She asked his forgiveness. She prayed. Then, it was her turn.

Fran was a little nervous. She went into the special room. At Fran's church, she could sit right beside Father Martin for this sacrament.

Father Martin greeted her with a smile and invited her to sit down.

Father Martin and Fran made the Sign of the Cross together. Then Father led a prayer. He read a little bit from the Bible about God's mercy and love and forgiveness. Fran listened.

After the reading, they were quiet for a short time. Fran told Father Martin her sins.

Father Martin asked Fran if she was sure that a certain thing she had done was a sin. Fran said she really wasn't sure. Father told her not to worry about it. She had only made a mistake. She hadn't done any wrong on purpose.

Father Martin told Fran that some sins were very hard to stop. He told her to pray to Jesus every day for strength. He also told her to ask Jesus' mother, Mary, to help her do what was good.

Then Father Martin gave Fran her penance. The penance would help her make up for the sins she had committed. Fran's penance was to play with her little brother for the next two days while her mother was fixing dinner.

After that, Fran prayed an Act of Contrition. She said, "Lord Jesus, Son of God, have mercy on me, a sinner." She told God she was sorry and would try not to do wrong in the future.

Then Father Martin gave Fran absolution. He told her that God forgave her through the Church. He put his hands over her head. This was a sign of God's forgiveness. The two of them said a prayer of thanksgiving together.

Father Martin and Fran said good-bye.

Fran felt good.

On the way home, she was even looking forward to playing with her little brother as a way of helping her mother at dinner time.

DOCTRINAL STORY

Jesus Came to Save Us

Jesus brought good news to the world.

He said, "I have come to save you from sin. Be sorry for your sins. God loves you and forgives you. God has given me the power to forgive sins."

Many people believed in Jesus. They were sorry for their sins. Jesus forgave them.

He made them happy sons and daughters of God again.

They tried hard to follow the way of Jesus.

Some people did not believe in Jesus. They did not want to follow his way. Some of them did not want other people to follow him either.

They feared Jesus and his message. They put him to death on a cross.

But death cannot destroy Jesus.

Jesus rose from death to a new and more wonderful life.

Jesus sent the *Holy Spirit* to Peter and the other Apostles. The Holy Spirit gave them great power.

They preached the *Good News* of Jesus.

The Apostles baptized people and brought them into God's family, the Church.

Jesus gave the Apostles other sacraments to help God's family. These sacraments are signs of God's love that really make a change within us if we are open to his love.

Jesus comes to help us in these sacraments. One of them is the Sacrament of Penance/Reconciliation.

Jesus gave the Apostles the power

to forgive sins. They forgave sins in the name of Jesus. The Apostles passed this power on to the Church.

Even today, after almost 2,000 years, the Church still celebrates the sacraments, signs of God's love working in us.

Soon you will celebrate the Sacrament of Penance/Reconciliation for the first time. You will have this sacrament to help you all your life. It is one of the ways that Jesus will help God's love grow in you.

THE RITE

Getting Ready for Reconciliation
I Examine My Conscience

I find a quiet place where I can think and pray.

I think about God's love for me.

I know that God wants me to be good.

I ask myself what I have done and said on purpose that is wrong.

These are the sins I will tell the priest about in my First Reconciliation.

Did I blame someone else for a wrong I did?

THE RITE

The Greeting
I Meet the Priest

I go to the reconciliation room. The priest welcomes me and helps me to feel good about coming.

I tell the priest that this is my First Reconciliation.

The priest and I make the Sign of the Cross, saying,

"In the name of the Father, and of the Son, and of the Holy Spirit. Amen."

The Sign of the Cross is a sign of Jesus' love. Can you make the Sign of the Cross? Can you say the words? Write them here.

_____
_____
_____
_____
_____
_____

THE RITE

Reading the Word of God
I Hear the Words of Jesus

The priest and I read together from the Bible.

We read how God is always ready to forgive.

We read about how much Jesus loves us.

> "Jesus said, 'Let the children come to me, and do not prevent them; the kingdom of heaven belongs to such as these.'… he placed his hands on them…."
>
> Matthew 19:14-15

IN THE LORD'S PEACE • LESSON 7

THE RITE

Confession of Sins
I Talk With the Priest

I tell the priest how I have acted selfishly and hurt others.

I confess my sins.

The priest asks me if I did these things on purpose.

The priest wants to find out if the things I tell him about are really sins.

Do you know when something is a sin? Read the examples below. Talk about them with your teacher or with a parent.

Example 1	Example 2
Mark's mother told him to carry out the garbage. Mark did not want to do it. He said, "Why don't you do it sometimes?" Then he went up to his room and played. Did Mark sin? What do you think?	Megan tried to help her mother feed the baby. But she dropped the baby's dish on the kitchen floor and broke it. Her mother said, "Oh, no! Now we'll have to get another dish." Did Megan sin? What do you think?

What three things make something a sin? Write them here.

1. _____
2. _____
3. _____

THE RITE

Accepting a Penance
I Will Try to Do Better

The priest helps me to be sorry for my sins.

I tell the priest that I will try to do better.

The priest gives me something to do, an act of kindness and some special prayers to help me be more loving.

The acts of kindness and the special prayers are called a penance.

Draw a picture of you doing something that will help you make up for wrongs and become a better person.

THE RITE

Prayer of the Penitent
I Say, "I'm Sorry"

I tell God I am sorry.
I say an Act of Contrition.
By this prayer I ask God's forgiveness.

I also ask for Jesus' help to always follow his ways and walk in his light.

Do you know an Act of Contrition by heart? Ask someone at home to hear you say an Act of Contrition. Write the words here.

_____
_____
_____
_____
_____
_____
_____

THE RITE

Receiving Absolution
I Receive Forgiveness

The priest forgives and blesses me in God's name.

He places his hands over my head.

He says, "I absolve you from your sins in the name of the Father, and of the Son, and of the Holy Spirit."

I answer "Amen."

Draw a picture of how you feel when you are forgiven.

THE RITE

Praising and Thanking God
I Go in Peace

The priest and I pray together.

We thank God for his love and mercy.

Then the priest tells me to "Go in peace."

I answer, "Thank you, Father."

Draw a picture showing how you will celebrate your reconciliation with God.

LET US PRAY

Dear Jesus,
We are ready now to celebrate the Sacrament of Penance/Reconciliation.
We are sorry for our sins.
We know that you love us all of the time.
We know that you have also given us a special way to show us your love and forgiveness.
It is the Sacrament of Penance/Reconciliation.
Thank you for this wonderful gift.

PRAYER

Afterward

You have celebrated the Sacrament of Reconciliation and have done your penance. Congratulations! Write a short prayer in this space. Try to say it every day.

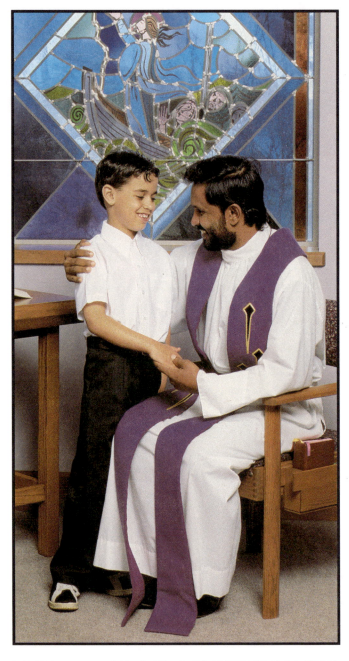

IN THE LORD'S PEACE • LESSON 7

FAMILY PAGE

This page is for you and your family to work on at home.

Ask the priest to sign his name below.

Ask all the other people who helped you celebrate to sign their names too. Some may add a message.

**Thank You for Helping Me Celebrate
My First Reconciliation**

_____
The date of my First Reconciliation

_____
The name of my parish family

FAMILY PRAYER

Dear Jesus,

We are proud and glad that _____ is ready to celebrate the Sacrament of Penance for the first time.

You love us all of the time, but this sacrament is something special.

Through your priest, you show us your love and give us your forgiveness.

You show us how to do better.

Thank you for this gift.

Thank you for this new happiness in our family. Amen.

THEME
Through his priest, Jesus helps us find forgiveness in the Sacrament of Penance. He died on the cross to make this forgiveness possible.

GOALS
As a result of this lesson, you and your child should:

1. Know that there are special times to ask forgiveness and to forgive one another — in daily prayer, in the Mass, and in the Sacrament of Penance.

2. Appreciate the Sacrament of Penance as a gift from God to his family.

3. Realize that Jesus is present in the Sacrament of Penance.

4. Realize that through his priest, Jesus helps you to find a way to make up for the hurt you have caused others or yourself; he helps you to forgive those who have hurt you.

5. Realize that the priest pardons you, not by his own power, but by the power of the Father, the Son, and the Holy Spirit.

6. Be glad for God's forgiveness and be willing to make up for the wrong you do.

7. Decide on some things you might do to avoid certain sins in the future and to develop attitudes and actions that will enrich your relationships with God and others.

MESSAGE
This final lesson gives your child immediate preparation for celebrating the Sacrament of Penance and for the communal penance service. It emphasizes that penance and reconciliation are possible because of the life, death, and resurrection of Jesus, who won new life for us on the cross and saved us from sin and death.

Prayers to Know

Sign of the Cross
In the name of the Father,
and of the Son,
and of the Holy Spirit. Amen.

The Lord's Prayer
Our Father, who art in heaven,
hallowed be thy name;
thy kingdom come;
thy will be done on earth as it is in heaven.
Give us this day our daily bread;
and forgive us our trespasses
as we forgive those who trespass against us;
and lead us not into temptation,
but deliver us from evil. Amen.

Hail Mary
Hail Mary, full of grace! The Lord is with you.
Blessed are you among women,
and blessed is the fruit of your womb, Jesus.
Holy Mary, Mother of God,
pray for us sinners,
now and at the hour of our death. Amen.

Glory Be to the Father
Glory be to the Father,
and to the Son,
and to the Holy Spirit.
As it was in the beginning, is now, and ever shall be,
world without end. Amen.

Apostles' Creed
I believe in God, the Father almighty,
Creator of heaven and earth;
and in Jesus Christ, his only Son, our Lord,
who was conceived by the Holy Spirit,
born of the Virgin Mary,
suffered under Pontius Pilate,
was crucified, died, and was buried.
He descended into hell;
the third day he rose again from the dead.
He ascended into heaven and sits at the right hand
of God, the Father almighty;
from thence he shall come to judge the living and
the dead.
I believe in the Holy Spirit,
the holy Catholic Church,
the communion of saints,
the forgiveness of sins,
the resurrection of the body,
and life everlasting. Amen.

Act of Contrition
My God,
I am sorry for my sins with all my heart.
In choosing to do wrong
and failing to do good,
I have sinned against you
whom I should love above all things.
I firmly intend, with your help,
to do penance,
to sin no more, and to avoid whatever leads me to
sin.

Revised Rite of Penance

Prayer to One's Guardian Angel

Angel of God, my guardian dear,
to whom God's love entrusts me here,
ever this day be at my side
to light and guard, to rule and guide. Amen.

Prayer Before Meals

Bless us, O Lord, and these your gifts,
which we are about to receive from your bounty,
through Christ our Lord. Amen.

Prayer to Know One's Vocation

Lord, what will You have me do?
Send forth Your Spirit into my heart so that I may know what Your will is for me.
I know, dear God, that I will find happiness only in doing Your will.
By doing Your will I will serve You, my God, and love my neighbor.
Speak to me, Lord, as I listen to learn Your will. Amen.

A Prayer Book for Young Catholics, Robert J. Fox